THE BEST DAMN ANSWERS to LIFE'S HARDEST QUESTIONS

A Flowchart Book

TESS KOMAN

illustrated by KATIE VERNON

WORKMAN PUBLISHING · NEW YORK

To my mom and dad, who are, like,
really excited about this little book.
Michael, the next one's for you.

—Tess

Text copyright © 2018 by Tess Koman
Illustrations copyright © 2018 by Katie Vernon

Library of Congress Cataloging-in-Publication Data is available.

ISBN: 978-1-5235-0145-8
Design by Becky Terhune

Workman books are available at special discounts when purchased in bulk for premiums
and sales promotions as well as for fund-raising or educational use. Special editions
or book excerpts can also be created to specification. For details, contact the Special
Sales Director at the address below, or send an email to specialmarkets@workman.com.

Workman Publishing Co., Inc.
225 Varick Street
New York, NY 10014-4381
workman.com
WORKMAN is a registered trademark of
Workman Publishing Co., Inc.

Printed in China
First printing July 2018
10 9 8 7 6 5 4 3 2 1

Introduction

God, everything is so depressing, amirite? This book, though, y'all—this book is not depressing. In fact, it's, like, the opposite! You want a little validation that another cup of coffee is warranted? I've got the correct—and only—answer for that (. . . it's "yes"). Need to know if calling out sick because you're hungover will forever taint your career like your mom told you it would? I've got a good answer for that as well (. . . it's "probably, but that's what unexpected personal days are for!"). How about some justification that, yes, bras are more irrelevant than most people on your least favorite dating app? Yep, there's an excellent answer for that one, actually (. . . it's "INDEED—GIRLS DAY!").

Finally, are you looking for confirmation that even *asking* all of the above doesn't make you a messy bitch or a terrible person, but instead just another #GrownAssWoman trying to make it in this messy, bitchy world? I've got the best damn answer for that, too (. . . it's "GIRL, THIS IS JUST *LIFE* NOW AND HONESTLY YOU ARE DOING **GREAT**").

Of course, getting to these answers isn't ever easy or fun, so here I am, trying to make your existential crises just a little bit easier and funner with some flowcharts and shit. It'll be great, I promise!

Let's fucking go.

Is A Bra Really Necessary?

2

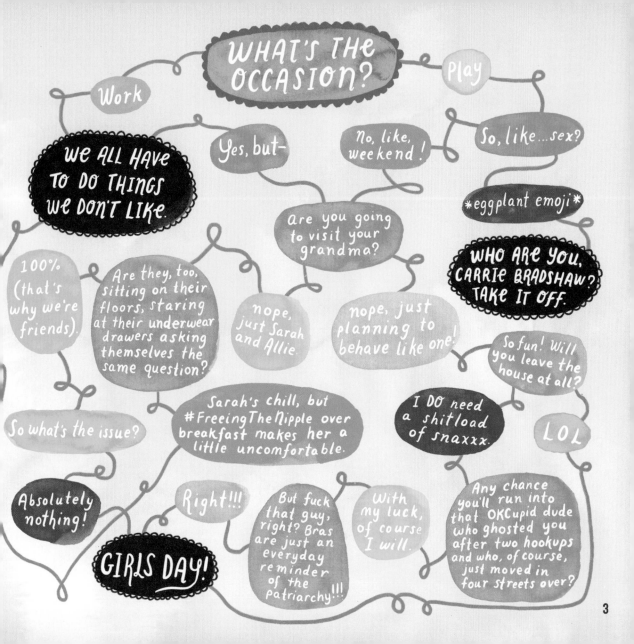

WHAT DO I EVEN WANT

WELL, THE QUESTION SHOULDN'T BE
"What do I even **WANT** to do with my life?"
BECAUSE THE ANSWER TO THAT QUESTION IS
"I WANT to QUIT EVERYTHING and OPEN
an AWARD-WINNING BAGEL SHOP CALLED
THE BAGEL SHOP

and it'll be SO GOOD PEOPLE WILL COME
FROM **SCHMEAR** and **FAR** to EAT THERE,"
hahaha, **OK**, I'M SORRY, WHAT WAS THE
QUESTION? **I LOVE BAGELS.** BUT AS FOR WHAT
I **SHOULD** DO WITH MY LIFE?

TO DO WITH MY LIFE?

I SHOULD certainly not DO A DEEP-DIVE
ON THE DEMOGRAPHICS OF
dark chocolate cream cheese.

DO PEOPLE REALLY EAT IT OR DO THEY JUST—nope,
NOPE! I SHOULD, AS A SELF-RESPECTING GROWN-ASS WOMAN,
SET concrete PERSONAL and PROFESSIONAL
GOALS AND WORK REALLY HARD TOWARD
THEM, WHICH WILL ULTIMATELY LEAD TO
HAPPINESS. So I Should be happy!
BAGELS MAKE ME HAPPY. Oh my GOD,
WHAT AM I EVEN DOING WITH MY LIFE???

5

DOES THIS NEED TO BE LOOKED AT??

WHAT IS THIS "THIS" YOU SPEAK OF?

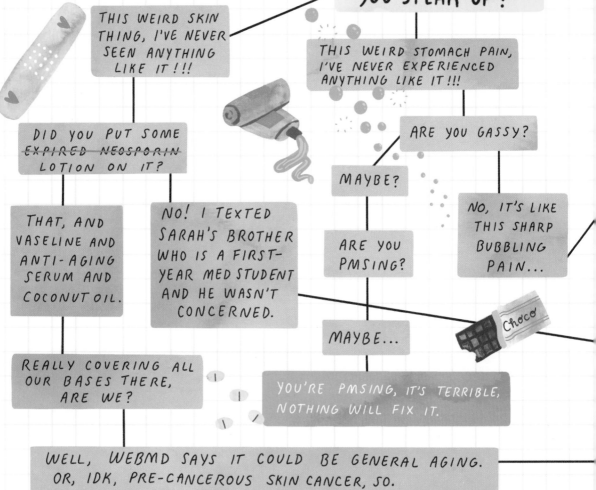

THIS WEIRD SKIN THING, I'VE NEVER SEEN ANYTHING LIKE IT!!!

THIS WEIRD STOMACH PAIN, I'VE NEVER EXPERIENCED ANYTHING LIKE IT!!!

DID YOU PUT SOME ~~EXPIRED NEOSPORIN~~ LOTION ON IT?

ARE YOU GASSY?

THAT, AND VASELINE AND ANTI-AGING SERUM AND COCONUT OIL.

NO! I TEXTED SARAH'S BROTHER WHO IS A FIRST-YEAR MED STUDENT AND HE WASN'T CONCERNED.

MAYBE?

ARE YOU PMSING?

NO, IT'S LIKE THIS SHARP BUBBLING PAIN...

MAYBE...

REALLY COVERING ALL OUR BASES THERE, ARE WE?

YOU'RE PMSING, IT'S TERRIBLE, NOTHING WILL FIX IT.

WELL, WEBMD SAYS IT COULD BE GENERAL AGING. OR, IDK, PRE-CANCEROUS SKIN CANCER, SO.

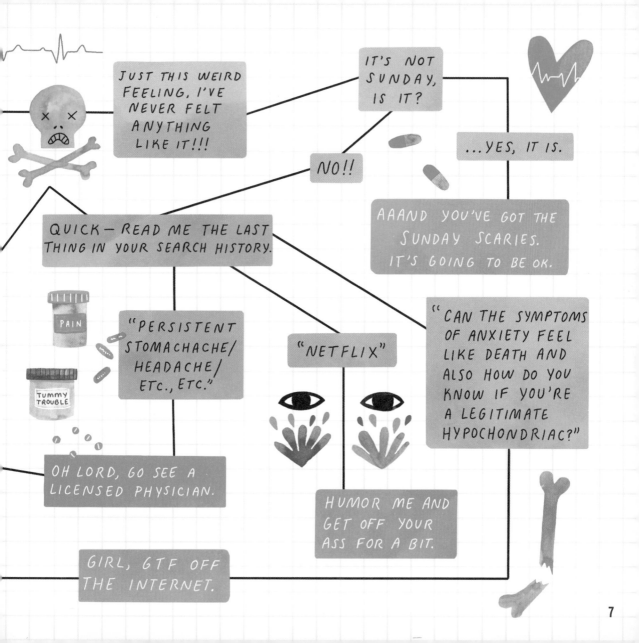

7

is everyone
mad at me?

SHOULD I COOK TONIGHT?

PROS

- You'll feel accomplished. You fed yourself, dammit!

- If you do it right, you can make enough leftovers for the week!

- Even if it looks sad, this is perfect fodder for a #homemade #foodie Instagram.

- You resolved to be better about spending your life savings on food.

- You can make a healthy and delicious meal that you'll feel good about eating!

CONS

- Time spent cooking is time not spent making a dent in your DVR build-up.

- Ordering food for four people would be easier and serve the same purpose.

- Your mom will like it. So will your aunt Debbie. No one else will like it.

- RESOLUTIONS MEAN NOTHING.

- You've got four boxes of Girl Scout cookies in your apartment. Let's be real.

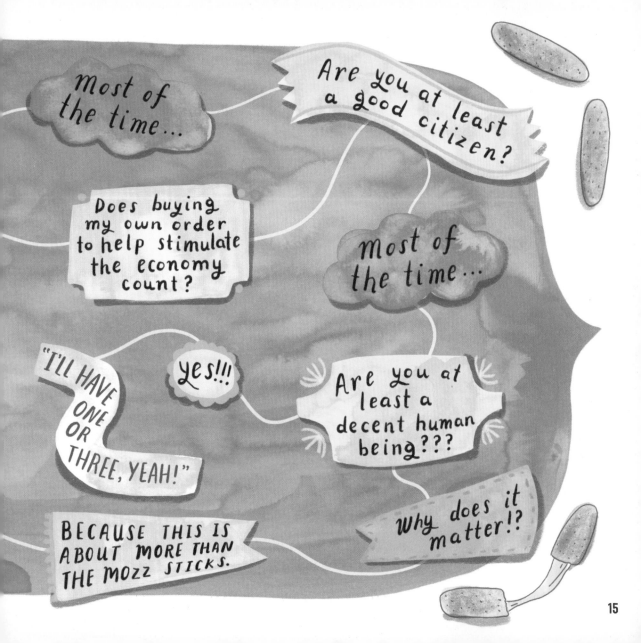

15

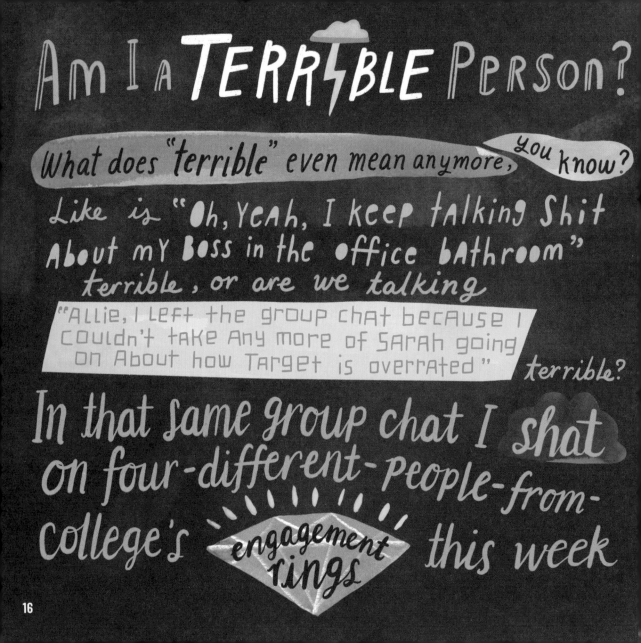

Am I a TERRIBLE Person?

What does "terrible" even mean anymore, you know?

Like is "Oh, yeah, I keep talking shit about my boss in the office bathroom" terrible, or are we talking

"Allie, I left the group chat because I couldn't take any more of Sarah going on about how Target is overrated" terrible?

In that same group chat I shat on four-different-people-from-college's engagement rings this week

and followed each comment with

"OMG DON'T MIND ME I'M TERRIBLE" AND "LOL WHATEVER, I'M TERRIBLE,"

but everyone else was like "haha OMG same,"

so is the real question

HAVE I SURROUNDED MYSELF WITH TERRIBLE PEOPLE WHO'VE MADE ME TERRIBLE?

OR AM I JUST TERRIBLE?

I'M NOT TERRIBLE, RIGHT? I'M NOT TERRIBLE...!

(you're not terrible.)

"Should we get brunch tomorrow?"

Just curious—what time is it?

11 a.m.

Are you currently at brunch?

no, but I HAVE to be productive tomorrow.

Nah, just bored at work.

mhm

Have you been drinking?

IT'S BRUNCH, OK?

"OMG YES, I LITERALLY CAN'T WAIT."

Just eating. A lot of eating.

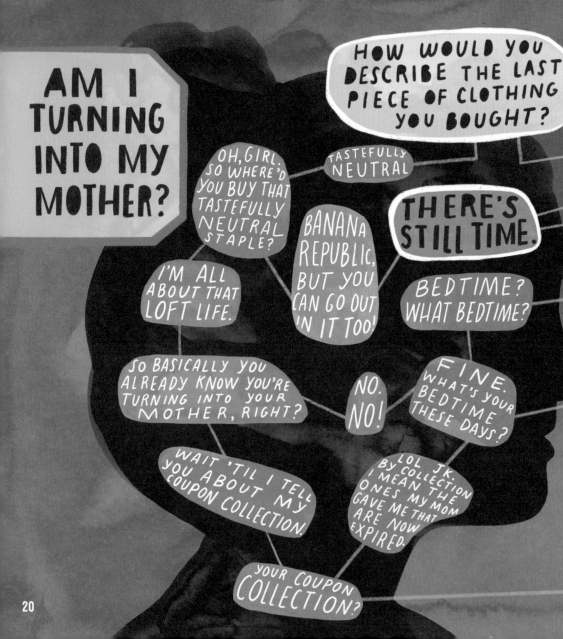

21

The man I LOVED in high school just proposed to

Do you still love him a little bit?

I'm always going to love him at least a <u>little</u> bit!!

That's #real.
But also remember
how high school was
disgusting??

Haha yes,
high school was
D.I.S.G.U.S.T.I.N.G.

NO! It wasn't
really SO
bad!!

OK. Yes.
Phones off.

THERAPIST
IT IS!

AND SO WERE HIGH
SCHOOL BOYS! YOU
HAVE ACCESS TO
GROWN-ASS MEN
NOW! FUN!

How about we just
turn our phones off
together for a sec?
It'll be so fun!

NEVER. I BLEED BLUE LIGHT!!!

his GF and it's all over the internet—NOW WHAT?

Literally no. But still!!!

Did you try your six meditation apps?

I bought $24.99-worth of new ones in the last hour.

I WILL NOW.

And you're still weirdly unsettled as shit?

yuuuuup

DON'T WORRY, THIS IS JUST THE OVERWHELMING SENSATION OF TIME PASSING YOU BY WHILE YOU COMPARE YOURSELF TO OTHER PEOPLE. IT'LL SUBSIDE IF YOU TAKE A XANAX!

Sad is a better word for it.

Time to text Sarah or your therapist.

Do I need another LBD?

PROS

- I will wear it!

- It's different from the others!

- I'll have it for years!

- It's an investment!

- It's so flattering!

- I need it!

- Once. Before Sarah borrows it and "forgets" where she put it.

- Slightly. It's black and short and tight and chafe-causing.

- Approximately one year, tbh. You'll unearth it next October from the base of your chair laundry mountain.

- Sure. It's cheap enough that you can turn it into rags after a few wears.

- Right. Like all the others!

- FINE.

A "NOW THAT'S WHAT I CALL MUSIC!" BINGE-LISTEN. TO LIVE ON LUNCHABLES AND WARHEADS. THE REVIVED JUICY TRACKSUIT!! FOR THINGS TO BE HOW THEY USED TO BE, BASICALLY.
IF YOU COULD HOP IN A TIME MACHINE TO 2007, WOULD YOU FEEL ANY BETTER?
NOT UNLESS THAT GENIE ALSO HELPED ME MEET MY PROFESSIONAL GOALS I CAN'T BELIEVE I HAVEN'T MET YET. AND HELPED ME STOP COMPARING MYSELF TO OTHER PEOPLE. AND TOLD ME EVERYTHING WAS GOING TO BE OK!
COULD I STAY THERE FOREVER?
OH HELL YEAH, THIS IS HAPPENING.
WHAT? NO.
WELCOME TO THE "EVERY ADULT EVER" CLUB, YOU BETCH.

Should I chop it all off?

I just want to do something different, you know? Like, not red-lips-instead-of-nude-lips different, but different enough that people will be like "OMG, you look different today! Your haircut! It looks great. No, I'm not just saying that, you look amazing."

A super-cropped cut is like the perfect way to do that, right? A mega-chop is basically a millennial forehead news ticker, declaring confidently "YOU ARE SPEAKING TO A GROWN WOMAN SO CONFIDENT IN HER GROWN-UP-NESS THAT SHE VOLUNTARILY CUT HER HAIR WITH WHIMSY AND CHILDLIKE FUN.

SHE REALLY HAS HER SHIT TOGETHER."
Though that whole shtick gets old
fast, doesn't it? And didn't I declare
on my 16th birthday that I would
never again revisit the hairstyle
I had when I was 8 years old?
And change is great and all, but
actually my hair grows slower than
back-to-back Hulu commercials and it's
an exhausting process. So is figuring
out what to do with an entirely new
head of hair each morning.

Layers are fun!
Layers would be different!

Do you remember how to read?
HOW RUDE!
I KNOW TO ANSWER "YES" WHEN NETFLIX ASKS IF I'M STILL WATCHING.
GO READ A BOOK SO YOU CAN PASS THIS DEPRECIATING SKILL ON TO YOUR ROBOT BABIES ONE DAY.
WHY MESS WITH A GOOD THING?
HAPPY WATCHING, FRIEND.

SNACK TiME?

PROS

- All the best things snack contantly: cute YouTube hamsters, squishy babies, healthy people.

- It's not just for my sake, but for others' as well: 9 out of 10 doctors agree—hanger is inconsiderate.

- It's the perfect time to sneak in "healthy" foods, like froyo or pretty juice!

- The aforementioned snacks also happen to be very 'grammable.

- Once you eat all the snacks, you HAVE to restock!!!

CONS

 "Constantly" does not mean every half hour.

It's also an incredible asset: no one fux with Hangry Me. Once I'm sated, I lose my edge.

It's a slippery "healthy" snack slope.

Are you even hungry or have you just not had a good food 'gram in a few days?

Once you eat them all, you are snackless. Sans snack. Without snack! WITHOUT FOOD. Oh god, food shopping while hungry is so fun.

Vibrator DEAD.

Lazy. Bored. Options?

Are you open to other options besides sleep?

I am!

Meh

THIS HAS BEEN FUN!

great! How about...

a hermit's treat yo'self

an orgasm a la 2004

a luxurious poop

pray tell—what's that?

1. DIY face mask
2. light candles
3. Spend rent $ making that Amazon Prime account worth it

that thing when you rearrange your pillows however it used to work for you and quietly get to it.

a lug-ZHUR-ee-us POOP: the biannual unhurried bowel movement that occurs only when your apartment is clean, quiet, and empty for once.

DONE + DONE.

OMG #TBT, FUN!

YES. THIS. I WANT THIS.

Oh god, am I as #millennial as they think I am?
HAVE YOU EVER...
Dropped your phone in an acai bowl from the chair you were standing on to photograph it?
no!
but you've held up a starving squad for a selfie, no?
OK, that's not fair.
I lost my last iPhone to a pitcher of mimosas.
Overheard an older relative call you a "foodie"?
They call anyone who's ever posted a food photo a foodie.
Ugh, foodie is offensive, I prefer "gourmand."
YOU ARE EXACTLY AS #MILLENNIAL AS EXPECTED.

"Hated everything"?
Posted a pic of just yourself at a wedding with the caption "loved celebrating with the happy couple!"?
who hasn't?
No! Just pictures of me with the happy couple.
yes, but I looked—
DON'T LET THE BABY BOOMERS STOP YOU FROM DOING YOUR THANG.
Hey! Just because my generation is more attuned to our feelings doesn't mean you can stereotype us!!!
STOP IT, YOU ARE WORSE.

SHOULD I BUY A PLANT?

PROS

- On a responsibility scale from 1-10, a succulent is 5 points below a dog and 10 below a child.

- Unlike other living things, a lil cactus would be harder to kill by accident.

- Caring about something other than yourself and who's creeping on your Hulu Plus account would be something to be proud of.

- Still, it might put her off the casual "when I have grandkids" comments for a while.

- It doesn't have to be a cactus! It could be an orchid! Or one of those baby palm trees the Property Brothers say liven up a room! Or a piece of turf for the entryway!

- It would be something to come home to at the end of the day.

CONS

- It is still a responsibility.

- But you **CAN** kill it. With love. With too much water. With not enough water, because you were scared to over-water it.

- "Oh, honey," your mom will say, vaguely alarmed and concerned about the enthusiasm of your selfless announcement.

- The comments might increase in desperation and urgency as she envisions a future of babysitting cacti.

- You will kill an orchid. You will kill a baby palm tree. You will simply not go buy a lone piece of turf. Who does that?

- It's not edible. What _IS_ edible? Hibiscus? Actual vegetable plants? Note to self: Buy food.

MY NEIGHBOR WON'T COOL IT WITH HER MUSIC. NOW WHAT?

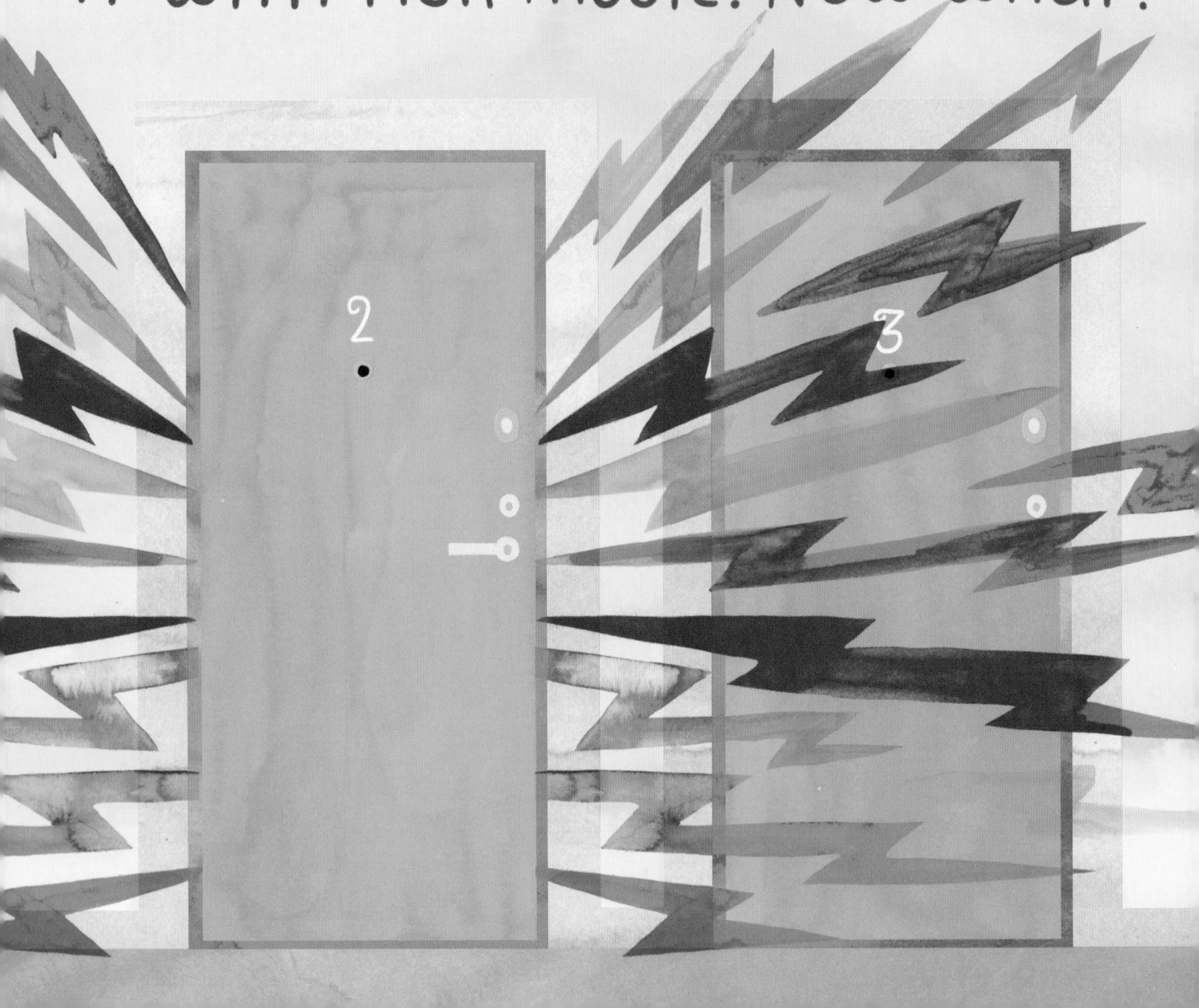

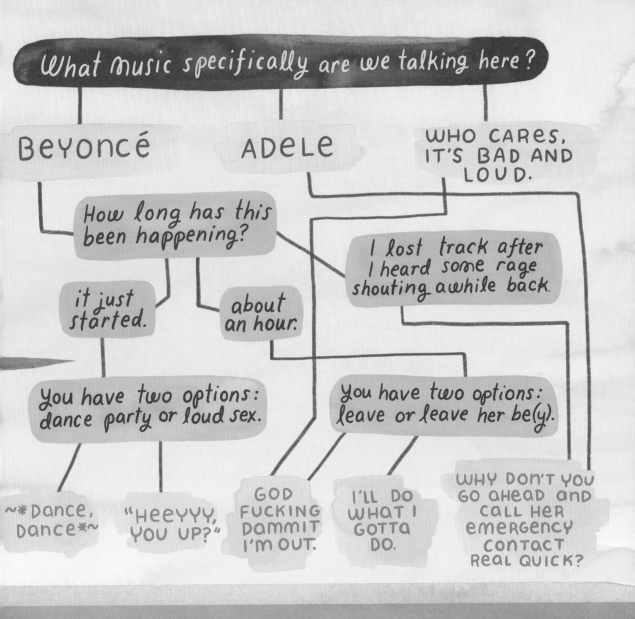

SHOULD I TEXT *THAT PERSON* ?

DO YOU ALREADY KNOW THE ANSWER?

Should Tina and Amy be the only award show hosts ever?

maaaybe

no!

WHATEVER. WHY DON'T YOU TAKE A LONG BATH WITH SOME FIFTY SHADES-ESQUE EROTICA INSTEAD?

...so you're craving human contact but don't want to make the effort?

DON'T YOU DARE TEXT THAT PERSON.

no!

GET AFTER IT.

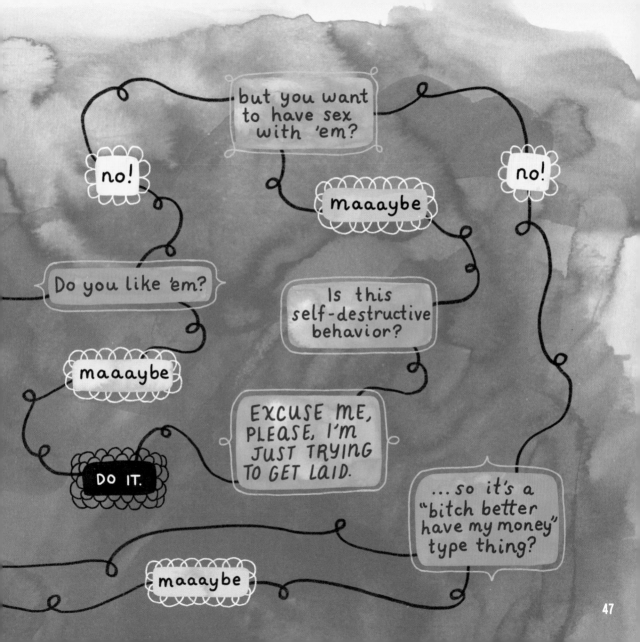

IS IT WORTH MAKING AN EFFORT TODAY?

It's not like I promised myself I'd get my **ASS TO THE GYM** today.

Well, I did, but who even keeps promises to themselves, you know? So that doesn't cou—oh, fuck.

You know, now that I think about it, I did spend a lot of money on that five-pack of Change-Your-Life-by-Lying-on-a-Yoga-Mat meditation classes. And I said I would go to those when I really didn't feel like making an effort.

But I also said I'd make an effort to **TALK LESS SHIT** about people when I graduated from college and look how that turned out, so.

Though I guess I could call Sarah while I walk *toward* the studio and talk about all our friends using backhanded compliments and then make a game-time decision about whether or not to "meditate."

That's making **hella** effort all around, no?

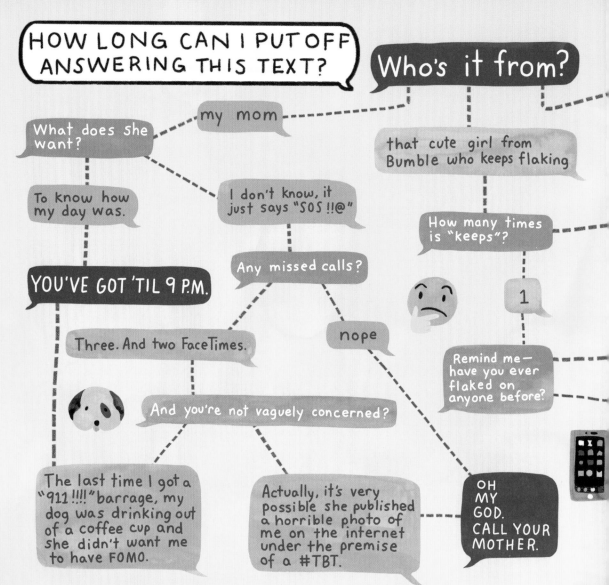

54

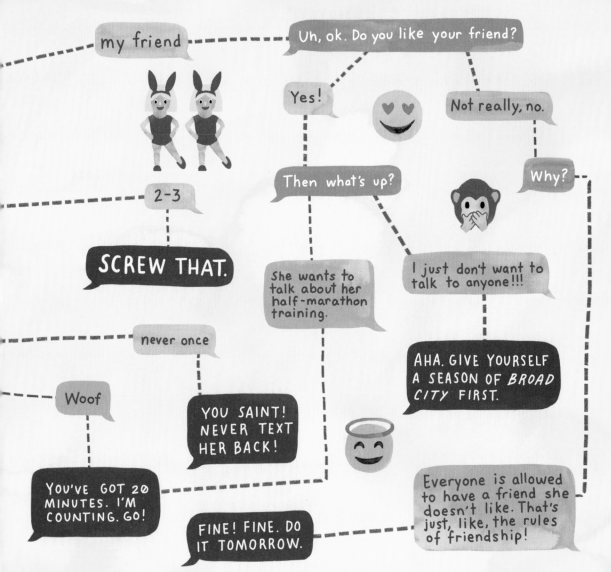

SHOULD I THROW OUT EVERYTHING I OWN?

My therapist once told me that if I identify the root of my anxieties, it will help me better understand my urges to make changes like this. So I *could* blame my temptation to trash all my shit on my ex being a total asshole, but I really don't want to give him the high honor of Sole Source of My Anxiety today.

It could be that I spent half of this month's rent on new jeans in every color as an effort to control my directionless life and now I actually have no room for them, but that would be too obvious. What if this anxiety is nothing but an indication that I'm ready for the next step of my life, which is adulthood by way of cleanliness? Or — OR! Adulthood by way of philanthropy? Donating, like, half of my earthly possessions is some Bill Gates-type shit. Yes! Yes. I'm going to woman the fuck up and Gates this place. I am next-level instigating change. I am great. I am not at all anxious about this decision.

She threw an orgy the one weekend I asked her please not to.
EVICTION
She went ahead and ate my stupidly expensive gluten-free bagel chips, too.
Without asking?
No, she asked.
Without asking.
Actually, she is.
Let it [MANCHE] GO.
DAIRY FOR DAIRY. FIND HER ICE CREAM. LET IT MELT.

Is 9 p.m. too early to go to bed?

you know the answer is no, right?

I know, it just feels too early.

Does it? Really?

It does!

... Why?

It just does! I can't justify it, I just feel like, as a functioning member of twentysomething society, I should be up until at LEAST midnight every night.

... but why?

Is this sad desk salad worth it?

Yet again, I find myself at a crossroads. After a late evening capped with night cheese, I am here at my desk with what doesn't even qualify as a sad desk salad. It is a bed of limp lettuce topped with chicken chunks and a light vinaigrette. A vinegar chicken lettuce lunch. I know I never pack a sad desk salad without a dairy-based dressing, but last night's cheese frenzy got a bit out of hand, rendering me useless this morning. **WHO AM I?** Am I really thinking of eating this? Are people who voluntarily eat things like this inherently better than I am? I could soldier through, become one of these superior desk salad people, or I could just... not.

And be happy.

buy more night cheese!

Should I get involved in
[X social media phenomenon everyone's talking about]?

PROS

People would enjoy hearing what I have to say about this.

Regardless, awareness is what's important, right? Like who's to say Blurry Selfies for Underappreciated Millennials isn't the new Ice Bucket Challenge?

I know exactly what to post to break the internet... with wokeness.

Not posting is like not voting. It's just not true to say one opinion can't make a difference!

Social media is an incredible tool for social activism.*

CONS

People? Your aunt Debbie, sure, but "people"?

Underappreciated Millennials don't want your blurry selfies. They want your attention.

The internet is an ever-filling cesspool of "fresh perspective" and nothing is original anymore.

One woman's blurry selfie is another five women's reason to unfollow her.

*Feeling better about how you spend a large fraction of your time on the internet.

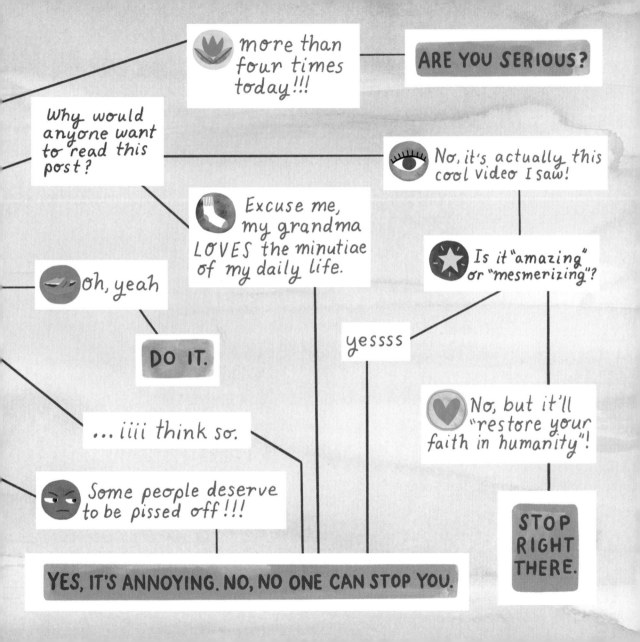

PROS

- I could be confident I don't smell like oft-sat-in couch.

- I could be confident I don't look like a crumpled accordion.

- I could reclaim the areas that used to be my floor and closet.

- I could make my roommate and parents proud to know me.

- I could finally have clothes to wear.

CONS

- I'd have to fold shit.

- If I don't have my daily "hahaha, rough morning, amirite?" bit, what will I talk about with my coworkers??

- Floor and closets are for basics, who needs them?

- I fed and dressed myself this whole week, what more could they possibly want?

- The yoga pants from high school that I've been living in don't count?

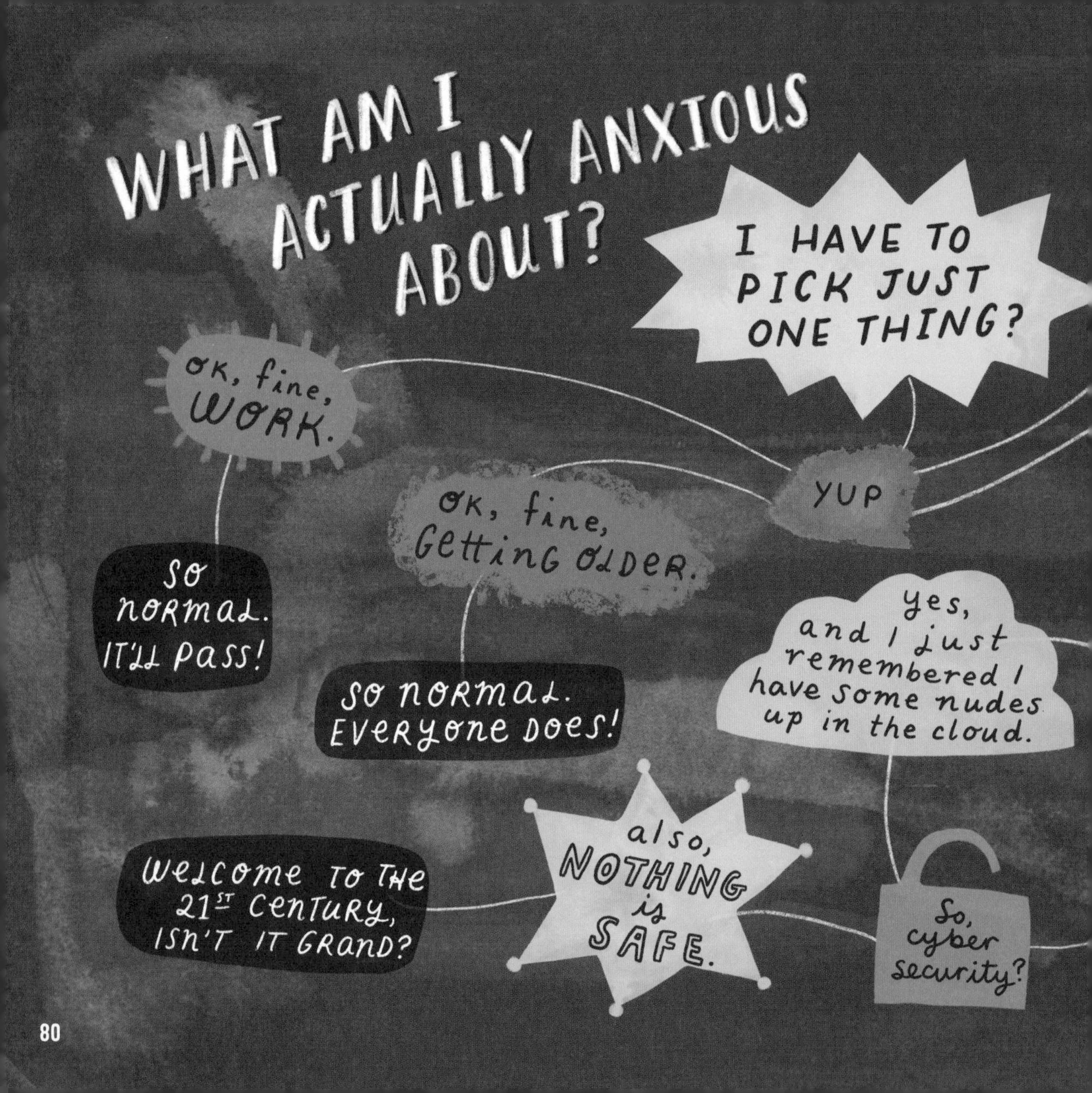
WHAT AM I ACTUALLY ANXIOUS ABOUT?
I HAVE TO PICK JUST ONE THING?
ok, fine, WORK.
So normal. IT'll pass!
yup
ok, fine, Getting older.
So normal. Everyone does!
yes, and I just remembered I have some nudes up in the cloud.
So, cyber security?
also, NOTHING is SAFE.
Welcome to the 21st century, isn't it grand?

THE END of the WORLD!!
um, ok, care to elaborate?
OK, fine, DYING ALONE.
So NORMAL. YOU MIGHT!
Did you know our jobs will be made irrelevant by smart-ass robots, in, like, five years? DID YOU? HM??
Today is the HOTTEST day of all time!
So, the rise of automation and advancement of technology?
So, global warming?
yes, and I have to change all my passwords.

Should I splurge for the more expensive bottle?

OK, this is just ridiculous. I am far past my Two Buck Chuck days, my "what is your cheapest bottle of moscato?" days (aka my prime). If you think about it, $30 is not a lot of money to spend on alcohol, especially not when you drink it in...two sittings. People order $15 glasses of wine all the time!

And they're not thinking "oh god, should I have finally subscribed to the *New York Times* and bought enough pita chips and hummus for the week instead?" Also, Sarah told me the more expensive the bottle, the less painful the hangover, and I don't know if I believe that, but I *do* know I deserve to treat myself.

Though if I had a dollar for every time I thought I deserved something, I'd have enough money to fund the third *Sex and the City* movie. So...won't the $19 bottle taste the same as the $30? Yes. No! No. I deserve this. It's done.

Should I cancel my plans?

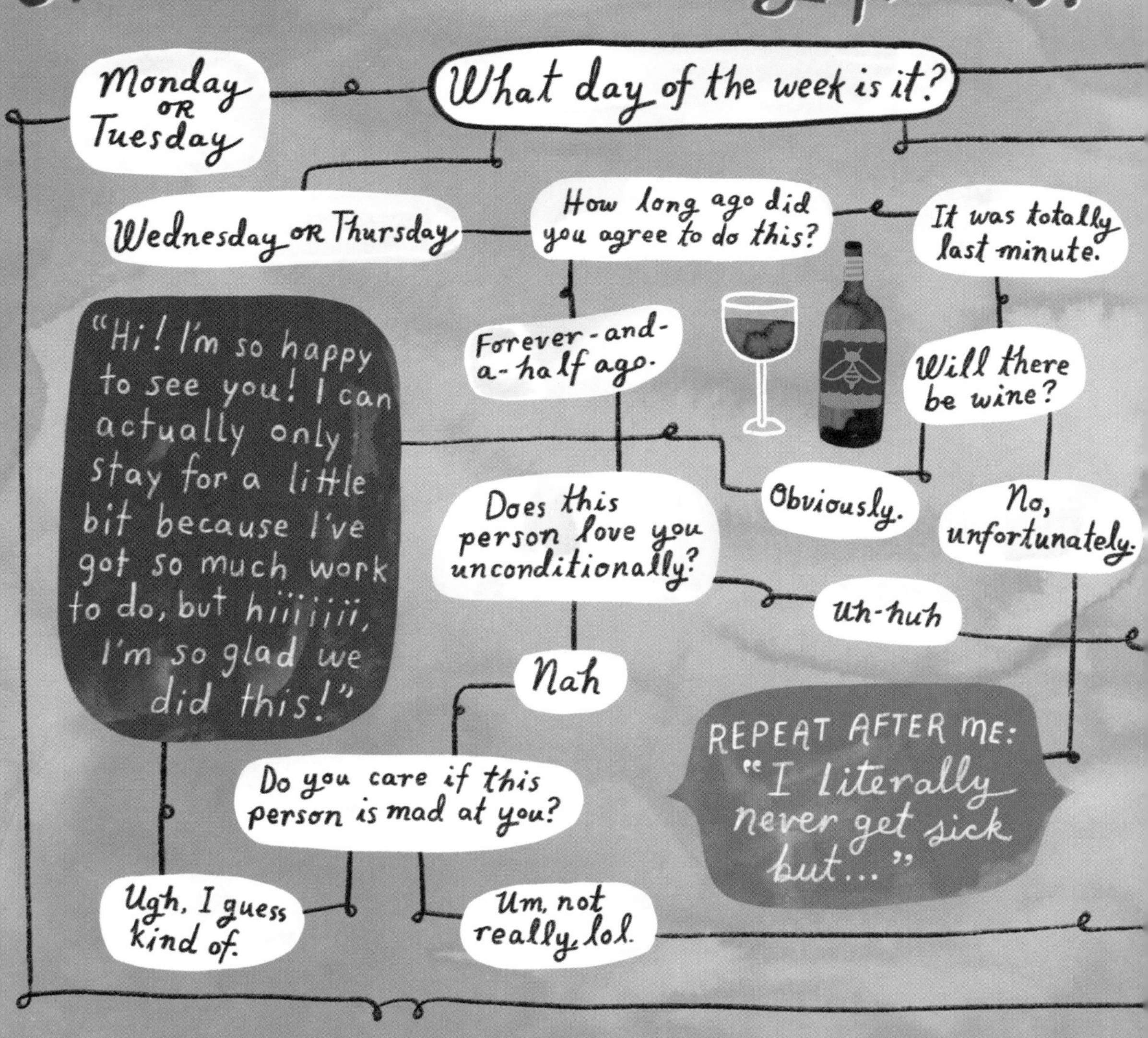

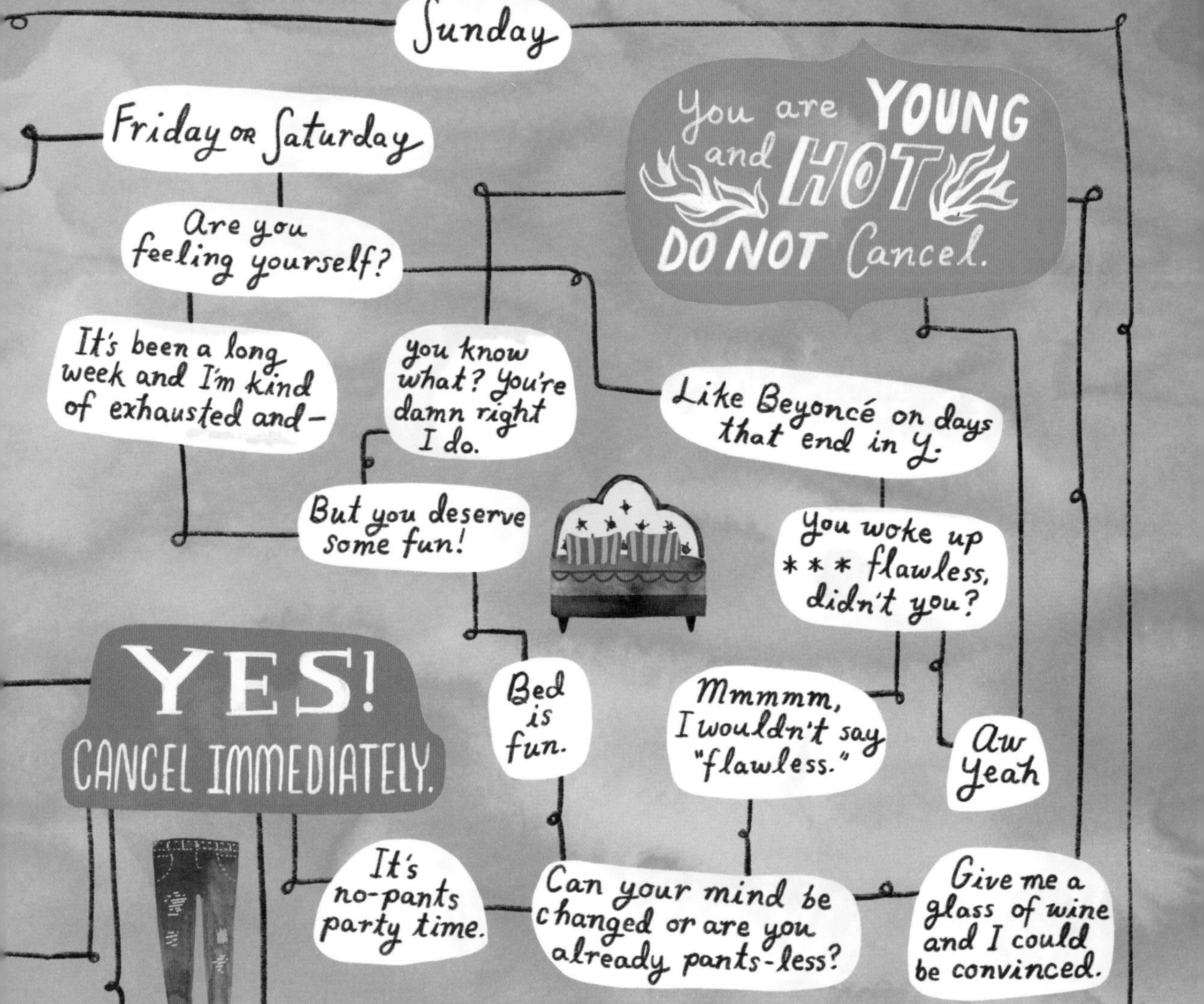
Sunday
Friday or Saturday
You are YOUNG and HOT DO NOT Cancel.
Are you feeling yourself?
It's been a long week and I'm kind of exhausted and—
you know what? You're damn right I do.
Like Beyoncé on days that end in Y.
But you deserve some fun!
You woke up *** flawless, didn't you?
YES! CANCEL IMMEDIATELY.
Bed is fun.
Mmmmm, I wouldn't say "flawless."
Aw Yeah
It's no-pants party time.
Can your mind be changed or are you already pants-less?
Give me a glass of wine and I could be convinced.

HE WANTS TO KNOW IF YOU'RE UP

PICK THE EMOJI SEQUENCE THAT BEST DESCRIBES YOUR MOOD.

ARE YOU?

And what's gonna help you deal with that?

"HEY BOY HEY."

um, excuse me, why is there no vibe emoji??

Because we live in an inherently sexist society that assumes women need men's help with E.V.E.R.Y.T.H.I.N.G.

BUT YOU DON'T, DO YOU?

No! and for orgasms? HELL no!

YOU CAN DO it ALL BY YOURSELF.

Should I commit to having a productive weekend?

LET'S DEFINE PRODUCTIVE...

 dealing with your nails, eyebrows, mustache, etc. **SURE!**

 masturbating **INDEED!**

→ hate-stalking, doesn't matter who **ABSOLUTELY!**

 tricking Sarah into revealing her Spotify Premium Password  **TOTALLY!**

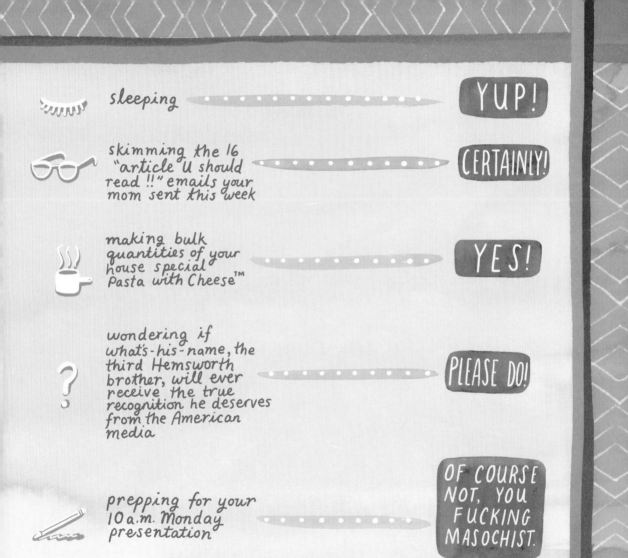

I'm not so sure.
Could you sit through The Hangover Part II with this person?
Could be fun!
Oh god no.
Could you do outdoor activities with this person? Like, camping or some other gross thing?
nope. nope. nope.
wouldn't be so bad!
What about a transatlantic flight with only this person and a broken in-flight entertainment system?
FIND A NEW PERSON.

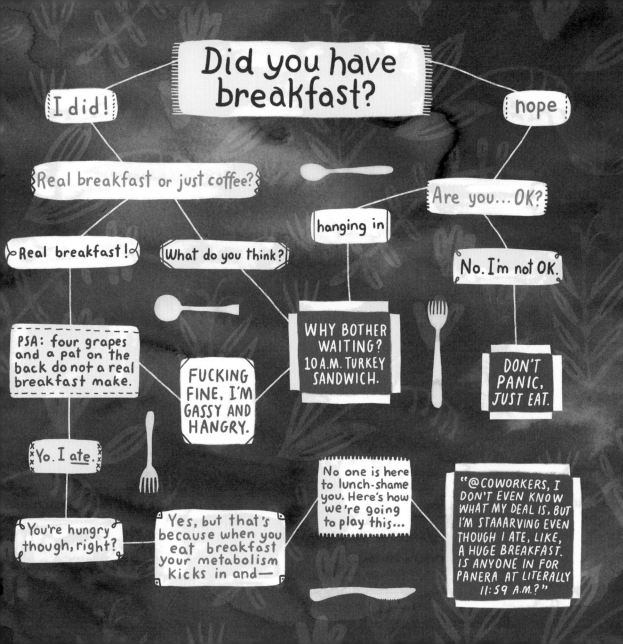

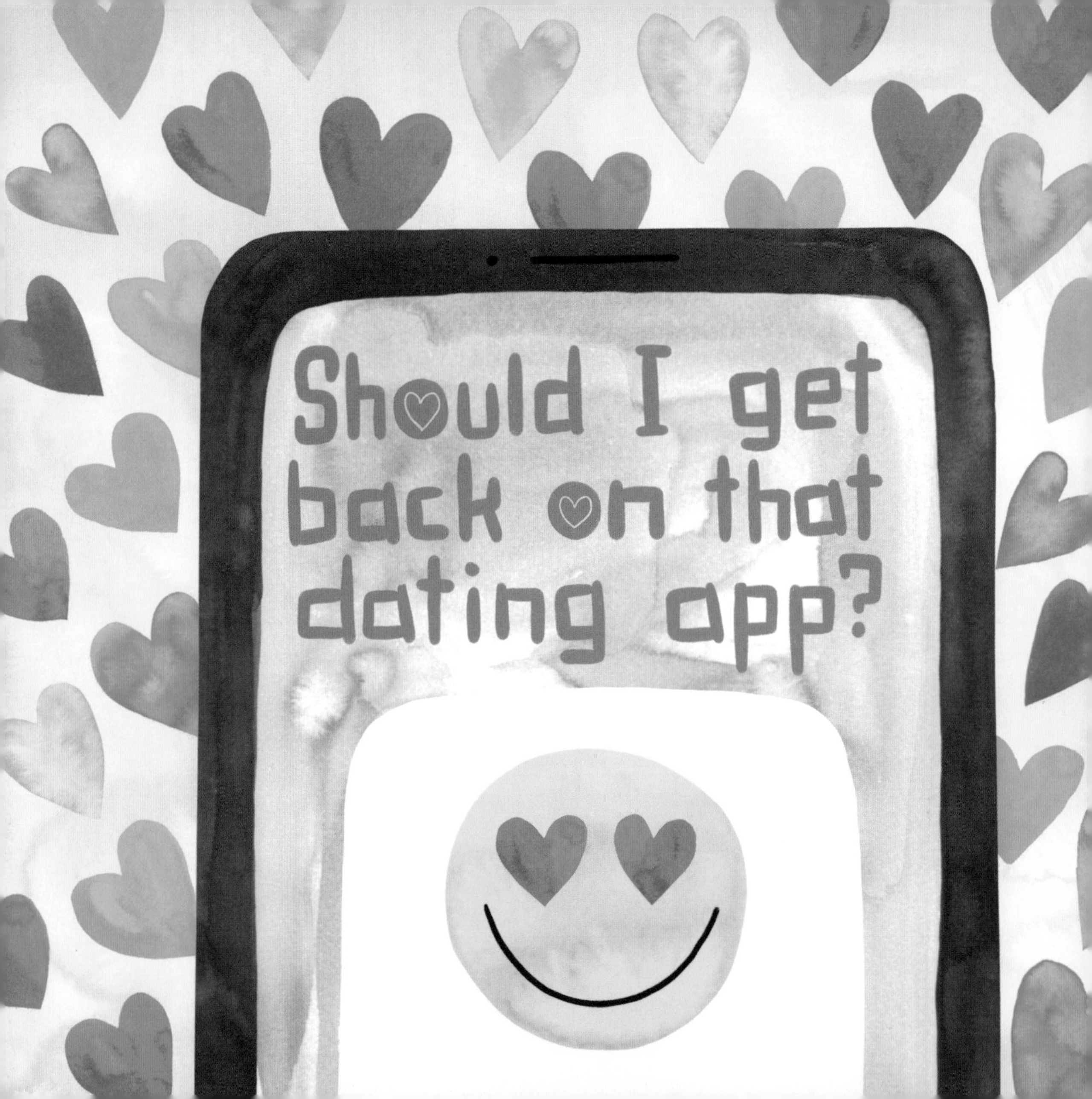
Should I get back on that dating app?

PROS

♥ It's a good way to meet people, and I haven't met many people lately.

♥ At the very least, I could make some new friends.

♥ ...or find fellow insomniacs to talk to when literally no one else is awake.

♥ .....or find people who I might not necessarily have anything in common with, but will make for interesting conversation.

● .... or find the same three motherfuckers in this one-block radius who inspired me to delete this goddamn app in the first place.

CONS

● People are disgusting and should be avoided at all costs.

● "

● "

● "

● "

DO I NEED TO LEAVE THE HOUSE TODAY?

PROS
OF STAYING IN

- It's the weekend, a prime opportunity to avoid any and all human contact.

- I can order food without talking to anyone! The internet is magical!

- I don't *need* pad thai! I can make do with pizza! Or dumplings!

- It's fine. I'm going to read my way through Oprah's Book Club pick from last year while eating PIZZA.

- I AM PROBABLY PERFECTLY CAPABLE OF AMUSING MYSELF FOR ONE NIGHT WITH PIZZA AND AN OLD FUCKING BOOK!!! RIGHT???

PIZZA

CONS
OF STAYING IN

- I don't have enough (good) food to last me 24 hours.

- That new pad thai place doesn't deliver yet. I would really very much like pad thai a lot.

- Neither of those things is pad thai.

- The bookstore that has this month's Oprah's Book Club pick is right next to the heavenly, delectable pad thai place.

- I NEED PAD THAI AND THE BOOK THAT MOST RECENTLY MOVED OPRAH TO TEARS IMMEDIATELY!!!

PAD THAI

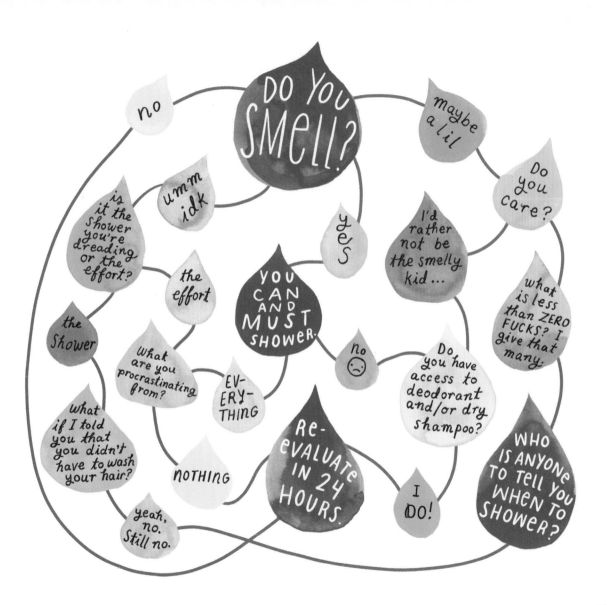

Should I attempt to make new friends?

How many BFFs do you have at the moment?

1

2-3

Do you have a dog you're obsessed with?

not yet

Do you often get that soul-swelling, satisfied feeling that only comes with the closeness of true friendship?

yes 😍

Do you, like, like the other people in your life?

not especially

of course!

The hashtag isn't "#NoNewFriend."

Nah, you're all good.

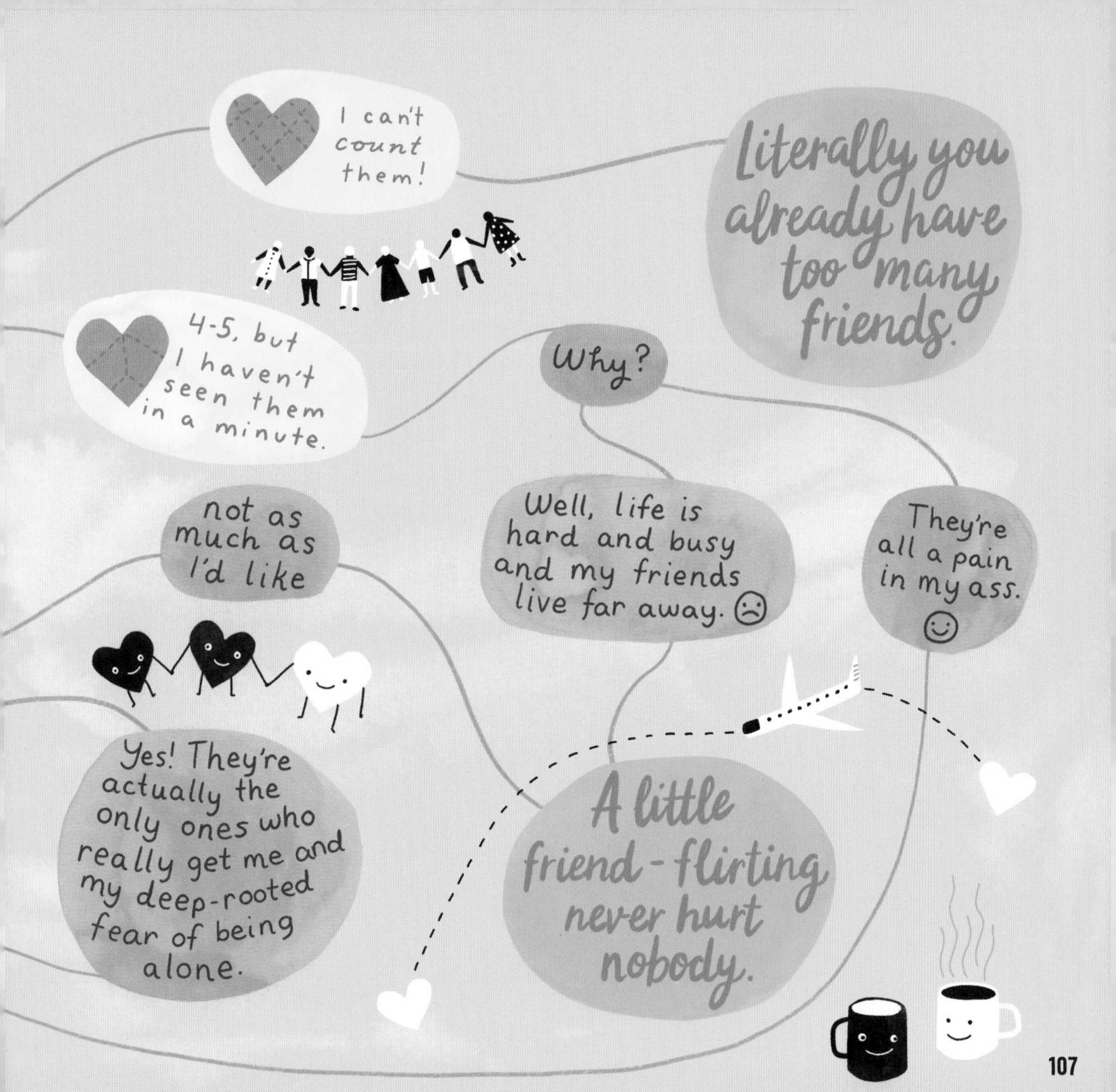
I can't count them!
Literally you already have too many friends.
4-5, but I haven't seen them in a minute.
Why?
not as much as I'd like
Well, life is hard and busy and my friends live far away. ☹
They're all a pain in my ass. ☺
Yes! They're actually the only ones who really get me and my deep-rooted fear of being alone.
A little friend-flirting never hurt nobody.

Why can't I just be old already?

I just want to be **75**, you know?
What even are the years between 25 & 74?
A stupid cycle of not understanding new
SNAPCHAT features but pretending you do?
A befuddling barrage of TIME HOP
notifications reminding you that you were
cute and lil on this day every year up 'til now?
A FACEBOOK flurry of marriages and
babies you're not having?
A very real resentment of anyone younger
than you?
A constant state of panic that you're
getting older and older until you lean
in to not giving a shit?
Yup. At the ripe old age of twentysomething,
I have realized time is terrible.
Fuck twentysomething.
I just want to be **75**... for, like, as many
years as possible.

Acknowledgments

Having worked on the internet for many years now, I realize the importance of keeping this sappy part brief. That said, it takes a village to make a baby's first book, so here goes: Thank you to my editor, Rachael Mt. Pleasant, who gave me this amazing opportunity, and everyone at Workman who helped make this book what it is. Tony Gardner took a huge chance on me as well, and for that I am the most grateful. To my very best friends (one of whom is NOT "Sarah"): Thank you for listening to and vetting for and loving me! Lunch League: You know why. Thank you to my beloved aunt Debbie, who was so excited about this book from day one . . . and will single-handedly fund book sales if need be. My parents deserve a thank-you, probably. They're kind of the best. My brother too. And Michael Todd Dolinger, who never wavers for a second: I fucking love you.

—Tess